Fantastic Finishes

By Jim Gigliotti

The Child's World
www.childsworld.com

The Child's World
www.childsworld.com

Published in the United States of America by
The Child's World®
1980 Lookout Drive • Mankato, MN 56003-1705
800-599-READ • www.childsworld.com

ACKNOWLEDGMENTS

The Child's World®:
Mary Berendes, Publishing Director

Produced by Shoreline Publishing Group LLC
President / Editorial Director: James Buckley, Jr.
Designer: Tom Carling, carlingdesign.com
Assistant Editor: Jim Gigliotti

Photo Credits:
Cover: AP/Wide World.
Interior: All photos by AP/Wide World except for
Corbis: 18.

**LIBRARY OF CONGRESS
CATALOGING-IN-PUBLICATION DATA**

Gigliotti, Jim.
  Fantastic finishes / by Jim Gigliotti.
    p. cm. — (The world of NASCAR)
  Includes bibliographical references and index.
  ISBN 978-1-60253-075-1 (library bound : alk. paper)
  1. Stock car racing—United States—History—Juvenile
literature. 2. NASCAR (Association)—Juvenile literature.
I. Title. II. Series.

  GV1029.9.S74G525 2008
  796.720973—dc22

                              2007049077

Contents

[OPPOSITE]
*Who won this fantastic finish between the
No. 29 car and the No. 01 car at the 2007
Daytona 500? Read on to find out!*

Ricky Craven was happy—and relieved—after pulling out the closest victory in NASCAR history.

1

Door-to-Door Racing

IT WAS LATE IN THE RACE IN THE CAROLINA
Dodge Dealers 400 at Darlington Raceway, and Ricky
Craven's No. 32 car pulled alongside Kurt Busch's No.
97 car. Craven had been trying to catch Busch for more
than 20 laps. Now, two laps from the end, he finally
did it.

Craven gave Busch a little nudge up toward the
wall, trying to get past. Busch wasn't going to give up
the lead if he could help it, so he nudged Craven back.
They came to the last lap door-to-door, zooming along
at more than 150 miles per hour. They bumped once.
Then again.

Down the stretch they came and across the finish
line—still side by side! Who won? It was so close that
no one in the stands or watching on television could
tell. Not even the drivers were sure. NASCAR officials

had to rely on an electronic timing device positioned at the start/finish line. It said that Craven won by .002 seconds—that's two-thousandths of one second! It was the closest race in NASCAR history.

It's hard to believe that after 400 miles (643 kilometers) of driving, only inches would separate the winners. It was a fantastic finish. But Craven's win was just one of many fantastic finishes in NASCAR history. Some of the others you'll find on the following pages.

While Craven's win was incredibly close, the races included here are not always the closest races. Sometimes they are races that are memorable for pitting different styles and personalities. Sometimes they are memorable for their historical significance. Or they are memorable for their impact on the season championship.

[OPPOSITE]
Craven (right) and Busch crossed the finish line just inches apart.

The list of races we talk about here is entirely **subjective**. Your favorite races may be different. That's the beauty of sports. Everyone sees the same thing, but we all see it a little differently.

2

Happy Days

[OPPOSITE]
The 2007 Daytona 500 had one of the wildest finishes ever. This crash took place just behind the leaders.

THE BIGGEST RACE IN NASCAR IS THE DAYTONA 500.
It's the race that every driver dreams of winning. For Kevin Harvick, his dream came true in 2007—but just barely! The race had an incredibly close finish that fans and drivers will be talking about as long as there is a Daytona 500.

Late in the race, a yellow flag came out after an accident involving several cars, including Dale Earnhardt Jr., Jamie McMurray, and Ricky Rudd. NASCAR uses different colored flags to send messages to its drivers. A yellow flag means caution. All cars have to slow down and stay in the same place that they were in when the flag came out. But you can see the problem if a yellow flag comes out very late in a race. By the time that the green flag is waved—green means "go," which in this case means the race is back on—cars could have completed the final laps and the race would be over. And that would be a boring way to end the day for both fans and drivers alike.

So several years ago, NASCAR started a system called "green-white-checkered finishes." It's a two-lap sprint to the finish in a race that otherwise would have ended under the yellow flag. The "green" means the race is back on and there are two laps left; the "white" means the race is on the last lap; and the "checkered," of course, is the **checkered flag** that comes out when the winner has crossed the finish line.

It was under the "green-white-checkered" system that the 2007 Daytona 500 restarted with Mark Martin

Early in the race, Kevin Harvick's pit crew worked hard to save him precious seconds—which came in handy later!

Fantastic Start

Anyone who saw the 2007 Daytona 500 will still remember it 50 years from now. That's the same way with the 1959 race.

The 1959 Daytona 500 was the first one in history. NASCAR founder Bill France Sr. had imagined holding an annual 500-mile race at the new Daytona International Speedway. But he never could have imagined the amazing finish in the very first one.

Lee Petty won the race—but not until several days after it ended. That's because the finish was so close that no one was quite sure who won. At first, officials said it was Johnny Beauchamp, who crossed the finish line at just about the same time as Petty. But then they said they would have to review pictures and TV footage to declare a winner. The trouble was that a third car driven by Joe Weatherly also crossed the line when Petty and Beauchamp did. Weatherly was one lap behind, but he was on the high side of the track, blocking the view of the judges.

Petty felt all along that he had won the race. He was right. Three days after the race, NASCAR determined that he had won by about two feet.

in the lead and Kyle Busch in second place. Harvick was back in seventh place. Busch tried to go to the right, but Martin blocked him; Busch tried to go to the left, but Martin blocked him again.

When the white flag came out, Martin was still in the lead in his No. 01 car. Harvick was in sixth place. Martin, a **sentimental** favorite of the fans, was trying to win the Daytona 500 for the first time in his 24th try. But while Martin was holding off Busch, Harvick came barreling by on the outside in the No. 29 car. "I was coming like a freight train," Harvick said.

Into the final turn they came, with Martin barely in front of Harvick. Suddenly, there was a huge wreck behind Martin and Harvick. Busch and several other cars were involved. Clint Bowyer's car even ended up upside down, sliding across the finish line on its hood!

But the race was over. Harvick had overtaken Martin by only inches to win. "Can you believe it?" the winner roared. Harvick, whose nickname is "Happy," was all smiles in Victory Lane.

Kevin Harvick won the 2007 Daytona 500 by sprinting to the finish line as fast as his car could take him. But would you believe that a driver once won a Daytona 500 going about 20 miles per hour (32 kilometers per hour) at the finish? That's right. David Pearson was going about as slow as a car moving through a school zone when he took the checkered flag at the 1976 Daytona 500. Here's what happened.

Pearson and Richard Petty (Lee Petty's son) traded the lead back and forth over the last 46 laps of the 200-lap race around the 2.5-mile (4-kilometer) oval track. That was nothing new. Petty and Pearson engaged in some classic head-to-head duels throughout their racing careers. They are two of the greatest drivers in NASCAR history. Both are members of the International

Unlike other sports, NASCAR's biggest event comes at the beginning of the year, not the end of the season. The Daytona 500 is run when all cars and drivers are fresh and ready to go.

Motorsports Hall of Fame. Petty's 200 race wins are more than any other NASCAR driver. Pearson's 105 wins rank second. They finished one-two in an incredible 63 races in their careers.

On the last lap, Petty was in front before Pearson zoomed past on the **backstretch**. Petty immediately tried to take the lead back by diving to the inside to pass Pearson again. Petty didn't get all the way past Pearson, though. The two cars were side by side briefly when they hit each other coming out of the final turn. "He went beneath me and his car **broke loose**," Pearson said. "I got into the wall and came off and hit him. That's what started all the spinning."

Petty spun wildly backwards, toward the finish line at first, then down toward the **infield** just short of the finish line. Pearson started off spinning toward the infield and

This photo shows how close the finish was between Harvick (29) and Martin (01) in the 2007 Daytona 500.

The Great American Race

They don't call it "The Great American Race" for nothing. The Daytona 500 not only is the most prestigious race in NASCAR, but it also often provides a fantastic finish.

We've already talked about a couple of great races in 1959 and 1976. There was another in 1979, when Richard Petty won after another last-lap crash. That wreck knocked out the two leaders, Davey Allison and Cale Yarborough (above). Petty zoomed by and was the first to the finish line, with Darell Waltrip on his bumper. Allison and Yarborough, meanwhile, got into a fistfight on the infield.

In 1999, 27-year-old Jeff Gordon took the lead late in the Daytona 500. But then he saw the black No. 3 car of Dale Earnhardt Sr. in his rearview mirror (left). Earnhardt's nickname was "The Intimidator." He tried everything he could to intimidate and get past the youngster over the final 10 laps, but he couldn't do it. Gordon won at Daytona for the first time after "the longest 10 laps of my life."

Two years later, Michael Waltrip held off Dale Earnhardt Jr. to win the Daytona 500 by about one-eighth of one second. The race ended in tragedy, though, when Earnhardt Sr. crashed in the last turn and was killed instantly.

14

hit another car. The second collision sent him spinning back toward the track. He had the presence of mind all the while, though, to engage the **clutch**. That way, he kept the motor running.

Pearson wanted to know if the race was over. Had Petty already crossed the finish line? His crew radioed that Petty hadn't reached the line, that he was stuck on the infield. "The King" was just 50 yards (46 meters) from the finish, but his car couldn't move. So Pearson put the pedal of his damaged car to the floor. He was going as fast as he could when his mangled car took the checkered flag—but it wasn't even as fast as the posted speed limit on a city street! "It seemed like I was a mile from the line and that it took forever to get there," he said.

Petty tried desperately to restart his engine as Pearson neared the finish line. But Petty couldn't get his car started in time, and he finished second. Pearson won the Daytona 500 for the first and only time in his career in what might have been NASCAR's most fantastic finish ever.

Richard Petty didn't win the 1976 Daytona 500, but he did win NASCAR's biggest race a record seven times.

3

The President and "The King"

RONALD REAGAN, THE PRESIDENT OF THE UNITED States, was on hand to watch the Pepsi Firecracker 400 at the Daytona International Speedway on the Fourth of July in 1984. In the end, though, the day was fit for a king—Richard "The King" Petty, that is.

The President's plane was still on the way when the race started. So from a phone in the plane, Mr. Reagan called out the traditional words to start the race: "Gentlemen, start your engines!" Ninety minutes later, the sight of the President's plane landing while the race was in progress was incredible. The massive **Air Force One** touched down just outside the wall beyond Turn 2 as cars raced past.

Mr. Reagan watched the rest of the race from a private box. It was the first time that a sitting President of the United States had ever gone to a NASCAR race. He

[OPPOSITE]
Richard Petty takes the checkered flag for the record 200th time.

President Reagan witnessed one of NASCAR's greatest finishes at the 1984 Firecracker 400.

was there, though, hoping to see what most of the fans in the crowd were there to see, too. They wanted Petty to win the 200th race of his career.

With 199 career victories, Petty already was the all-time leader. No one else was even close. But he really wanted to get to 200, and had been stuck on 199 for several weeks. It looked like this might be the day when he held the lead with just three laps to go. Just one small problem: Cale Yarborough was close behind.

There was a crash, however, on the 158th lap. Neither Petty nor Yarborough was involved, but the yellow caution flag came out. The caution rules at the time were different than they are today. Back then, drivers maintained the position they were in once they pass the flag stand. Other drivers slowed down after they had taken the yellow caution flag. Being far ahead, though, Petty and Yarborough passed the stand before the yellow flag came out. So they could keep racing until they passed the stand again. "Racing to the caution" is

Cale Yarborough was a three-time season champ, but he couldn't deny Petty his historic victory.

Clever Like a Fox

Richard Petty's dramatic victory in the 1984 Pepsi Firecracker 400 came exactly 10 years after he was on the losing end of another of NASCAR's most fantastic finishes. It was the 1974 Firecracker 400, when David Pearson edged him in the annual race on the Fourth of July. (The race is now known as the Pepsi 400, and falls near, but only occasionally on, July 4.)

Pearson used a bit of trickery to beat Petty that day in 1974. It was the kind of move that helped earn him the nickname "Silver Fox."

Pearson led Petty on the final lap of the 160-lap race at Daytona. Pearson couldn't pull away from his rival, however, so he figured that second was the place to be. That's because if the driver in second place was close enough, he could sit in the **draft** of the car in front of him. Then the second-place car would "slingshot" past the leader. This used to be the favored technique on fast tracks such as Daytona and Talladega (in Alabama).

Pearson wanted to be in second place going into the final turn. So he slowed down and moved his car to the left, toward the infield. Petty, the spectators, and the media all thought something was wrong with Pearson's car. Did he have engine trouble? Maybe a flat tire?

Petty zoomed past. There was nothing wrong with Pearson's car, though. He quickly got back to speed and moved up behind Petty. Coming out of the last turn, Pearson pulled out from behind and shot past Petty to win by one car length.

Pearson's move was risky, but dramatic. At first, Petty was upset because he felt like it could have caused a crash. In the end, though, "The King" admitted that he wished he had thought of it first.

what it was called, and it's illegal now. Instead, the field is "frozen" in the order the cars are in when the yellow flag comes out.

But in the Firecracker 400, both drivers knew what was at stake. With only two-plus laps to go, the race was sure to end under the caution flag. (Again, the rules have been changed now to a "green-white-checkered finish.") So Petty and Yarborough floored it. They knew whoever led at the end of the 158th lap was going to be the winner of the race. It was a sprint to the lap line.

Yarborough (left) and Petty fly to the finish. This is what they call "door-to-door" racing!

The two drivers dashed around the track. First, Yarborough shot past Petty's famous number 43 on the backstretch. Petty quickly moved to the inside and drew back alongside Yarborough. It was door-to-door racing at its most exciting. Petty and Yarborough flew toward the flag stand at nearly 200 miles (322 km) per hour. They bumped once, twice, three times. "The last 'bam' sort of squirted me ahead," Petty said.

That was just the edge he needed. Petty crossed the flag stand barely ahead of Yarborough. His 200th victory was secured. Because the race ended under caution two laps later, there is no official margin of victory credited. The actual margin, though, was about the width of a fender. That's how close it was when Petty and Yarborough crossed the lap line.

President Reagan told Petty after the race that he'd never seen anything like it. "The King" was thrilled that his record win came on July 4 with the President in attendance. "I couldn't have asked for a better time," Petty said.

4

Fight to the Finish

[OPPOSITE]
Kurt Busch couldn't be sure he would raise the championship trophy until the final race was over.

THINK OF THE STOCK-CAR SEASON AS ONE LONG, grueling race. At the end of that race, NASCAR's season champion is awarded the Sprint Cup. (In past years, it's been known as the Winston Cup or the Nextel Cup, depending on the award's **sponsor**.) We've already seen that NASCAR races can have some fantastic finishes. So it figures that lots of times, the entire season wraps up with a fantastic finish, too.

Take 2004, for instance. That year, Kurt Busch entered the last race of the season in Homestead, Florida, with an 18-point lead in the standings. Since the winner of the race would get 180 points—and even last place would get 34—that wasn't nearly enough of a lead. Especially with Jimmie Johnson, Jeff Gordon, Dale Earnhardt Jr., and Mark Martin all close enough to take the championship with a big finish.

This was the first year of NASCAR's playoff chase. That's when the season standings are reset 10 races from the end to create a "playoff" format. The new system created just the excitement that NASCAR hoped it would. Only a few places up or down in the final race could determine the winner of the Nextel Cup.

On the 93rd lap of the 271-lap Ford 400, Busch's wheel broke. The tire came flying off. Busch kept himself

Never Give Up!

Kurt Busch and Alan Kulwicki never gave up even when it looked as if their championship hopes might be out of reach. All NASCAR drivers also know they should never give up even when it seems the checkered flag might be out of reach—because you never know what might happen.

The best example of that came in the 2000 Winston 500 at Talladega Superspeedway. Talladega always has been known for some wild action, but this day was wild even for that track. The lead changed hands 46 times among 21 different drivers. One of those men was Dale Earnhardt Sr., but he found himself in 18th place with only five laps to go. That's when Dale Sr. made a charge that will always be remembered. In three laps, he moved all the way up to fourth place. His son Dale Earnhardt Jr. and two other drivers were all that stood between him and victory. That wasn't about to stop "The Intimidator." Dale Sr. zoomed by to win.

Dale Sr.'s victory came on the same track on which he rallied from 23rd place with 13 laps to go in the 1984 Talladega 500.

from crashing, but by the time he got his car fixed, he was in 28th place in the race—and out of first place in the overall standings.

Lap by lap, the overall standings changed. Johnson gave himself a chance to win the Nextel Cup by finishing second in the Ford 400 to Greg Biffle. But Busch never quit. Slowly, he moved up in the race. With 56 laps to go he was in 20th place. With 21 laps left, though, he made his move to seventh. Now he was back in the lead in the overall standings. He finished the Ford 400 in fifth place, which was good enough to clinch his first Nextel Cup. "It's an unbelievable deal," Busch said after the race. "This is what a team does to win a championship. They persevere on a day such as this."

With each lap of the Ford 400, the season standings seemed to change. At the end of the day, however, Kurt Busch (97) was the man in front.

Alan Kulwicki's 1992 championship marked the last time an owner-driver won the season title. The cost (in both time and money) of running a team is so high today, he might be the last one to ever do it.

Before Busch's winning margin, the closest championship race was in 1992. And just like in 2004, the title chase that year had more twists and turns on the last day than a NASCAR **road course**.

That year, Davey Allison entered the last day of the season leading in the points race. He needed to finish in fifth place or better at the final race to clinch his first title. But with 74 laps to go, Allison crashed. He finished 27th in the race—and too far behind to take the season title.

That left Alan Kulwicki and Bill Elliott to battle for the championship—as well as for the checkered flag in that same race. The crews of both teams were frantically adding up points to see who would come out on top. In the end, they knew that if Elliott won, Kulwicki had to lead more laps in the final race to win the championship. (NASCAR awards a five-point bonus to the driver who leads the most laps in a race.) So Kulwicki planned his **pit stops** to make sure he led the most laps. In the end, it worked. Elliott won the Hooters 500, but Kulwicki won the Winston Cup. He led 103 laps in the final race, while Elliott led 102. Because Kulwicki got the bonus points and Elliott did not, Kulwicki won the championship by 10 points. "I won, but I lost," Elliott said.

Whether it's one amazing race or one long season, in NASCAR, as they say in baseball, "It's never over 'til it's over!"

Time Line

1959 Lee Petty is officially named the winner of the inaugural Daytona 500 three days after the race is run

1974 David Pearson fakes car trouble and allows Richard Petty to pass him on the last lap of the Firecracker 400, setting up a late pass

1976 David Pearson limps across the finish line ahead of Richard Petty's stalled car after a last-lap crash in the Daytona 500

1979 Richard Petty wins the Daytona 500 while Davey Allison and Cale Yarborough brawl on the infield after a last-lap crash

1984 On July 4, Richard Petty wins his 200th race, the Firecracker 400, with President Reagan in attendance

1992 Bill Elliott wins the season-ending Hooters 500, but loses the season championship to Alan Kulwicki by just 10 points

1999 Jeff Gordon holds off Dale Earnhardt Sr. to win the Daytona 500

2000 Dale Earnhardt Sr. comes back from 18th place with five laps to go to win the Winston 500 at Talladega

2001 Michael Waltrip beats Dale Earnhardt Jr. by .124 seconds to win the Daytona 500, but Dale Earnhardt Sr. is killed in a last-lap crash

2003 Ricky Craven wins the closest race in NASCAR history, beating Kurt Busch by .002 seconds in the Carolina Dodge Dealers 400

2004 Kurt Busch wins the Nextel Cup in the closest season points race

2007 Kevin Harvick and Mark Martin stage a thrilling sprint to the finish in the Daytona 500; Harvick wins by inches

Glossary

Air Force One   the specially equipped plane that transports the President of the United States

backstretch   the straightaway part of a racetrack that's opposite of the finish line

broke loose   in racing, when a car breaks loose, the back end drifts to the outside of the track

checkered flag   the flag that signifies the winning car has crossed the finish line

clutch   a device that allows a car's driver to switch gears

draft   a pocket of air directly behind a moving car that acts like a vacuum (to a car that follows close enough behind it)

grueling   very tiring

infield   the area in the middle of a racetrack; many tracks have grass growing in the infield

pit stops   when a driver stops his car during a race for service, such as for a tank of gas or a tire change

road course   a type of NASCAR track that has many turns

sentimental   appealing to emotions or feelings

sponsor   a company that pays an athlete or a team to promote its products

subjective   based on personal feelings or opinions, not facts

Find Out More

BOOKS

Eyewitness NASCAR
By James Buckley, Jr.
DK Publishing, 2005
This photo-filled book takes you inside the world of NASCAR. See close-up pictures of engines and other gear, meet the heroes of the sport, and see more photos of pit-stop and racing action.

History of NASCAR
By Jim Francis
Crabtree Publishing, 2008
Take a wild ride through more than 50 years of NASCAR action—meet the top drivers and get a front-row seat to some amazing races.

NASCAR Record & Fact Book
Sporting News Books, 2008
This handy reference source is loaded with facts and figures about current drivers and NASCAR history.

Pit Pass
By Bob Woods
Readers' Digest Children's Publishing, 2005
Take an "inside" look at NASCAR tracks, drivers, cars, and gear.

Stock Car's Greatest Race: The First and the Fastest
By Phil Barber
The Child's World, 2003
Want to learn more about some of the greatest Daytona 500 races? This book will help fill you in.

WEB SITES

Visit our Web site for lots of links about NASCAR:
www.childsworld.com/links

Note to Parents, Teachers, and Librarians: We routinely check our Web links to make sure they're safe, active sites—so encourage your readers to check them out!

Index

ABOUT THE AUTHOR

Jim Gigliotti is a writer who lives in southern California with his wife and two children. A former editor with the National Football League's publishing division, he has written more than twenty books about sports and personalities, mostly for youngsters.